In 1848 a handsome young man of 18 was called on to rule the vast Austrian Empire. Over the next 68 years he would conscientiously go on with the tasks entrusted to him, despite a series of extraordinarily harrowing family tragedies. He was the Emperor Franz Josef; and not the least of his tragedies was his marriage to the enchanting Elisabeth of Bavaria.

# A CHOICE OF COUSINS

**AN AMBITIOUS ARCHDUCHESS HAD HER SIGHTS SET ON THE AUSTRIAN THRONE, GROOMING HER SON FOR THE ROLE. SUCCESSFUL IN THAT, SHE PLANNED A FAMILY MARRIAGE**

*♛ From the start, Archduchess Sophie had great ambitions for her eldest son, reflected in this joint portrait from 1832 above*

I N THE 19TH CENTURY, THE POWERFUL Austrian Empire ruled much of central and Eastern Europe. Franz Josef was born into the ruling family, the centuries-old Habsburg dynasty, on 18 August 1830. His grandfather, Franz I, was Emperor, but it was by no means certain that Franz Josef would one day inherit the imperial crown.

In 1835 the Emperor died and his elder son, Ferdinand – Franz Josef's uncle – succeeded to the throne. Ferdinand was epileptic and an invalid. It seemed unlikely that he would have any children. Next in line of succession was Franz Josef's father, the Archduke Franz Karl.

The Archduke was a commonplace man with no significant political ambitions, but his wife was made of sterner stuff. Disappointed in her marriage, the Archduchess Sophie concentrated all her hopes on Franz Josef, the oldest of her four sons. Under her supervision he was given an education designed to fit him to wear a crown – a crown that she was determined to get for him if she could.

## A sense of duty

Franz Josef repaid his mother's care with an intense devotion to her and a sense of duty that became his outstanding characteristic. He began his studies at 6 a.m. each morning. Over the years he learned several languages, including Hungarian and Czech, the tongues of two of the multi-national empire's most important peoples. His mother arranged that he should learn statecraft from the Machiavellian Austrian chancellor, Metternich – a man she detested, but whose political skills she was shrewd enough to appreciate.

If not brilliant, Franz Josef emerged from the process with a well-informed and well-trained mind. His boredom when confronted with literature or art, however, suggested that imagination and sensitivity were not among his strong points. Nevertheless, he looked every

inch a prince, growing from an attractive child to a strong, good-looking young man with a quiet air of authority. Franz Josef also became a fine sportsman, a passionate hunter and an accomplished dancer.

## Love of military order

A rather different side of Franz Josef's personality was revealed in his preoccupation with things military. On his fourth birthday he was given his first set of toy soldiers and became an enthusiastic collector, soon acquiring models representing every Austrian regiment. At 13 he was appointed a colonel with a live regiment of his own, and in his adult life he wore military uniform almost all the time. Curiously, this obsession did not make Franz Josef yearn to be

*♛ The Archduchess had a forceful personality and an overwhelming allegiance to the values and lifestyle of the Habsburg court. She brought up her children strictly, overseeing their studies and leading them in their prayers above*

*An Evening Prayer/Fendi, Graphische Samlung Albertina*

## 'Physically and morally fearless'

REPORT ON FRANZ JOSEF

a conqueror, but contributed to the love of order, hierarchy, method and routine that would come to dominate his existence, making him a dedicated desk-soldier.

Soldiers played a decisive part in the crisis that was to make Franz Josef Emperor. In 1848, revolutions broke out all over Europe. In the Habsburg dominions themselves, revolution in Austria and nationalist risings by the Emperor's Hungarian and Italian subjects broke out almost simultaneously. Franz Josef served with the army in Italy, proving himself 'physically and morally fearless', before joining his family in Vienna.

In August they were forced to flee from the city, owing their lives to the 7,000 troops who

be all right.'

Over the following three years the crisis was overcome, the revolution was suppressed and, with Russian help, the Hungarians were crushed. Secure at last, Franz Josef – or perhaps his mother – decided that it was time for the Emperor to marry. But the supply of eligible and available girls was unusually small, partly because Austria had fallen out with several European monarchies.

The most promising girl, Princess Anna of Prussia, was unimpressed by the Austrian Emperor when he visited Berlin, and declined to break a previous engagement to a lesser German Prince. Franz Josef's face was saved by an announcement that the Princess had been un-

## 'The only man in the family'

### COMMENT ON ARCHDUCHESS SOPHIE

♛ *The Habsburg monarchy dominated central Europe in the mid-19th century, taking in the whole of modern Austria, Hungary and Czechoslovakia, as well as parts of Poland, Italy, Romania, Yugoslavia, and the USSR* left.

♛ *Most of Europe was convulsed with revolution in 1848; the French monarchy was overthrown, and a Republic was declared during fighting in Vienna* below

Royal Geographical Society

Hulton Picture Company

escorted them to Olmütz in Moravia. With the dynasty tottering, the Archduchess Sophie alone remained resolute; she was 'the only man in the family', said one observer.

### The new Emperor

Sophie succeeded in persuading the Emperor and his advisors that only a new image could save the Habsburgs. Consequently Ferdinand abdicated and the Archduke Franz Karl was passed over in favour of his own son, Franz Josef, who became Emperor without ever having been heir apparent. As Franz Josef knelt before Ferdinand, who was in all probability less feeble-minded than was commonly supposed, the former Emperor quietly told his nephew: 'God bless you, be steadfast and everything will willing to convert to Catholicism, the faith of the Habsburgs and most of their subjects.

It was at this point that the Archduchess Sophie, by birth a Bavarian Princess, wrote to her own family in Munich to propose that her sister Ludovika's eldest girl might make a suitable match for Franz Josef.

For Ludovika, this was a wonderful opportunity. While her sisters had married into the Austrian, Prussian and Saxon Royal Families, she had had to be content with her cousin Max, a fellow Bavarian who had blue blood but nothing in the way of regal prospects to recommend him. In fact, he was made a 'Duke in Bavaria' only as an act of courtesy to console Duchess Ludovika for her relative failure in the marriage market.

Another disadvantage of the match between Ludovika and Max was that it accentuated the inbreeding already so characteristic of Bavaria's ruling Wittelsbach dynasty. Sophie, Ludovika and Max and, of course, their respective children, were all descended from either Maximilian I, King of Bavaria, or from his sister. The effects of inbreeding ranged from eccentricity and nervous instability to outright madness, and would have tragic consequences for the next two generations.

Wittelsbach eccentricity was manifested in its most agreeable form in Duke Max, a charming, irresponsible and indiscreet character who wrote bad poems and plays, aspired to become a circus rider, and scandalized society by befriending bohemians and vagabonds.

Roger Viollet

Popperfoto

Roger Viollet

♛ *Though he had been well-schooled by his mother, and had performed valiantly in the Italian uprising that year, Franz Josef was still little more than a boy* above *when he ascended the Austrian throne in 1848*

♛ *After the Viennese uprising crumbled, the 18-year-old Franz Josef became Emperor in a ceremony in the Archbishop's Palace at Olmütz on 2 December 1848. Only members of his family, cabinet ministers and generals witnessed the valetudinarian Ferdinand handing the sceptre of power to his nephew* above. *Franz Josef's father, Franz Karl, stands beside him on the steps. He had been passed over as Emperor as he was tainted by the errors of the past. Austria needed a symbol of hope, and chose the dashing young man who had fought alongside the national hero, General Radetzky* left, *in the successful campaign against the Italian rebels*

He was also a far from faithful husband, although this fact did not prevent him from giving Ludovika nine children, five of them girls for whom it would be necessary to find husbands. For a family on the foothills of royalty this could have proved a serious problem. But if Ludovika's eldest girl, Helene, married the Emperor of Austria, the entire family would gain in status and all the sons and daughters would benefit.

## Grooming Helene

Understandably, when she received her sister's suggestion, Ludovika made frantic efforts over the next few months to coach, groom and dress Helene in an attempt to make sure that she would attract Franz Josef and live up to the Archduchess's exacting standards.

# 'There were times when she had literally to be tied to her chair'

### A GOVERNESS ON YOUNG SISI

None of this was of much concern to Ludovika's second daughter, Elisabeth, who was known in the family circle as Sisi. Three years younger than Helene, she was still little more than a girl, becoming 15 during the winter of 1852-53 when all the attention was focused on her sister. It was Helene who acquired an expensive wardrobe of furs and ball gowns, and also Helene who had the more doubtful privilege of taking lessons in French, history and (because Franz Josef was a dedicated equestrian) riding.

Meanwhile, nobody seems to have noticed that little Sisi, hitherto not especially pretty, was beginning to blossom into the beauty whose womanhood would capture an Emperor's heart and dazzle Europe.

## Carefree Sisi

Sisi – or Amelia Eugenia Elisabeth von Wittelsbach-Birkenfeld-Gelnhausen, to give her full name – was born on 24 December 1837, at Possenhofen, the castle outside Munich where the family lived. Unlike their grand Royal kinsmen, Duke Max's children had the scope to lead a relatively carefree existence.

Sisi, with her father abetting her on his infrequent appearances at home, saw as much of the woods and fields around the castle as she did of her tutors. She was already showing signs

of the nervous restlessness that was to become one of her most striking characteristics. One of her governesses later recalled that 'there were times when she had literally to be tied to her chair.'

However, although her formal education may have left something to be desired, Elisabeth had other advantages. As well as being beautiful she was charmingly spontaneous in her behaviour. She was tall, with a tiny waist

Munich Stadtmuseum

♛ *Duchess Ludovika already had two children, Helene and Ludwig, when Elisabeth was born in December 1837 above. There were to be five more. Elisabeth inherited her mercurial nature from her father, Duke Maximilian below, who made her his favourite*

Popperfoto

♔ *Elisabeth's elder sister, Helene right, was reserved and sensible, and thought by her mother and aunt to be a suitable bride for Franz Josef*

♔ *Elisabeth often accompanied her father on his trips around Possenhofen and on Lake Starnberger, where the quixotic Duke loved to play the zither below*

Österreichische National Bibliothek

and incredibly long auburn hair. Her carriage was graceful. And, unlike her sister, she was a superb, ardent horsewoman – a significant and conspicuous accomplishment in an age whose supreme aristocratic symbol was the thorough-bred horse.

## Romantic poetry

In spite of these apparently extroverted, social qualities, Elisabeth was highly strung and in-ward-looking, probably happiest and most at ease among the familiar faces at home. Here she wrote verses in a melancholy romantic vein, many of them addressed to a handsome, dark-eyed aristocratic neighbour, whom she wor-shipped at a distance, and perhaps mainly for purposes of literary inspriration. In the best romantic tradition, he departed and soon after-wards died.

Elisabeth continued to write poetry throughout her life, some of it genuinely self re-vealing. She shared this and other tastes with her father, whose favourite she was, and came out of herself in his company.

Together, father and daughter practised equestrian circus tricks in private, and engaged in at least one whimsical public prank. Passing themselves off as wandering musicians, Duke Max and Sisi entertained the local country folk with songs and dances. Whether or not they were fooled by the imposture, the audience good-naturedly demonstrated their apprecia-tion by throwing coins which Sisi, revealing a keen eye for open-air theatre, caught in her apron. Years later she is said to have shown a lady-in-waiting a handful of these, remarking

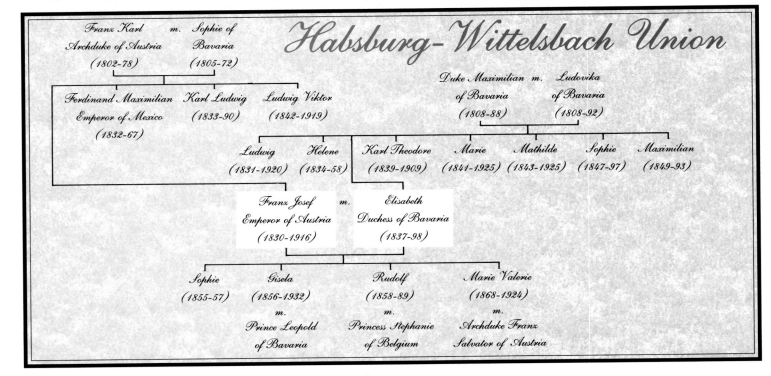

*Habsburg-Wittelsbach Union*

Franz Karl — m. — Sophie of
Archduke of Austria / Bavaria
(1802–78) / (1805–72)

Ferdinand Maximilian / Karl Ludwig / Ludwig Viktor
Emperor of Mexico / (1833–90) / (1842–1919)
(1832–67)

Duke Maximilian — m. — Ludovika
of Bavaria / of Bavaria
(1808–88) / (1808–92)

Ludwig / Helene / Karl Theodore / Marie / Mathilde / Sophie / Maximilian
(1831–1920) / (1834–58) / (1839–1909) / (1841–1925) / (1843–1925) / (1847–97) / (1849–93)

Franz Josef — m. — Elisabeth
Emperor of Austria / Duchess of Bavaria
(1830–1916) / (1837–98)

Sophie / Gisela / Rudolf / Marie Valerie
(1855–57) / (1856–1932) / (1858–89) / (1868–1924)
m. / m. / m.
Prince Leopold / Princess Stephanie / Archduke Franz
of Bavaria / of Belgium / Salvator of Austria

## THE BELOVED HOME

The future Empress Elisabeth was born at the castle of Possenhofen *right*, about 17 miles from Munich, and for the whole of her life it was probably the place closest to her heart. Despite its formidable appearance, Possenhofen was really a large, comfortable family mansion, with lawns and gardens where Elisabeth could run about barefoot, and a variety of pets and domestic animals for her to play with. Beyond lay woods and fields, the blue waters of Starnberger Lake and the snowy splendours of the Bavarian Alps – a setting that aroused Elisabeth's intense love of nature, and one to which she would return, year after year, when the cares of her imperial office became too heavy for her

that this was the only money she had ever earned by honest labour!

The grooming of Helene – a far less mercurial character – went on steadily. But any prospect of an immediate meeting with Franz Josef vanished in February 1853, when a Hungarian tailor's apprentice tried to assassinate him. Franz Josef received an unpleasant wound in the throat but he recovered quickly.

### Courting popularity

For the first time he actually became a popular figure with his people, especially when he insisted on driving in public without a military escort. The Viennese, who had previously found their new Emperor rather too dry and distant, admired the matter-of-factness with which he treated an attempt on his life. For monarchs, he would later declare, this sort of thing was simply an occupational hazard.

Archduchess Sophie decided that a Royal marriage, with all its romantic and ceremonial trappings, would set the seal on the Emperor's popularity. As ever, Franz Josef was ready to do his duty, and his encounter with Helene was finally arranged for the middle of August 1853.

### Family get-together

Although both parties were well aware of the business in hand, the meeting was decently disguised as a family reunion. Sophie, Ludovika and a third sister – Elise, Queen of Prussia – were there with some of their children, including Franz Josef and his Wittelsbach cousins.

Since Duke Max was unwilling or unable to attend, it was eventually decided that Sisi should go with her sister and mother to gain a little experience of the great world. Neither the Habsburgs nor Wittelsbachs dreamed that in doing so they were providing the young Emperor with a choice of cousins.

*By 1853, Franz Josef was beginning to grow into his imperial role below. Though Archduchess Sophie summoned his cousin Helene to Austria as a possible bride for her son, it was instead the wasp-waisted Elisabeth right who caught his eye*

*Franz Josef*

Suddeutscher Verlag

Archiv Fur Kunst & Geschichte

♛ Though his mother had ambitions for her eldest son, Franz Josef was not born to be Emperor. His grandfather, Franz I, was still on the throne. At the age of three he was painted *above* with his innocent face framed by a conventional mass of blond curls

♛ Under Metternich's tutelage, Franz Josef grew into a serious-minded youth, who took an interest in all things military *right*

♛ As soon as he was old enough, his mother began to prepare him for rule. She reasoned that his imbecilic uncle, Ferdinand, could not last long, and that her husband, next in line, was a dullard who wanted only to be left alone to hunt. She summoned the great statesman, Metternich, to teach Franz Josef, whose only boyhood companions were his younger brothers *above*

Archiv Fur Kunst & Geschichte

## Elisabeth

♛ **Elisabeth was showing signs of her charm and beauty even at one year old** left

♛ **Elisabeth** right *at four had only happy memories of her early life in the rambling, rather shabby family home at Possenhofen; a greater contrast to the staid and repressive Habsburg court could not be imagined*

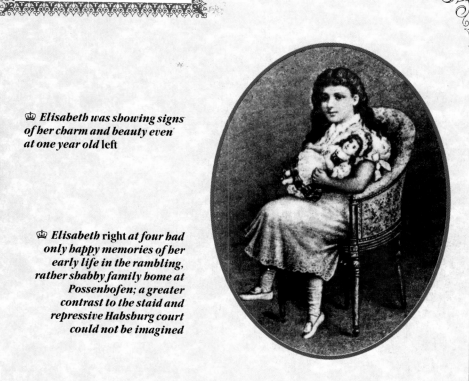

Bildarchiv Preussischer Kulturbesitz

♛ *The highly-strung, artistically-minded Elisabeth emerged from her undisciplined childhood as an aristocratic young woman* left *who wore her mane of hair up and posed demurely for the lithographer*

9

# CENTURIES OF TRADITION

*The Crown Jewels of the Austrian Empire and the subsequent Austro-Hungarian Empire have their origins in the Holy Roman Empire, founded by Otto I in the 10th century. King Frederick III of Habsburg was elected Holy Roman Emperor in the 15th century and the Habsburgs maintained their hold on the title until Napoleon dissolved the empire in 1806. Francis I of Habsburg, Holy Roman Emperor at the time, named himself 'Hereditary Emperor of Austria', founding a new empire which lasted until the Allies dismantled it in 1918*

Interfoto

Claus Hansmann

👑 The Imperial Coat-of-Arms *top* of the Austro-Hungarian Empire. The topmost crown, an emblem of the Austrian Empire, was made for Emperor Rudolf II in the 16th century. In the painting *above* Franz Josef wears, on a gold and emerald chain, the Order of the Golden Fleece, which was associated with the Habsburgs for centuries

👑 The Crown of Charlemagne *left* was never worn by him but was made in the 10th century for the Holy Roman Emperor Otto I and then re-modelled for Otto III, who added the gem-studded arch

Archiv Fur Kunst & Geschichte

The Imperial Orb *left* was fashioned in the late 12th century from gold inlaid with pearls and precious stones. It was used in the coronations of Holy Roman Emperors until the empire was abolished in 1806. Francis I fled with the orb to Vienna. His ancestors left it behind when driven out in 1918

Set in a gilded frame, a sepia-tinted photograph of Franz Josef, taken in 1890 when he was 60, forms the centrepiece of this Royal Family Order *above*. It would have been presented by the Emperor himself to favoured members of his family and perhaps, also, to his mistresses

Claus Hansmann

Mansell Collection

# ENCHANTING ROMANCE

**THE EMPEROR'S HEART WAS CAPTURED BY HIS YOUNG COUSIN AND THEY WERE SOON ENGAGED. HER FAIRY-TALE ENTRY TO THE CAPITAL AND A GLITTERING WEDDING DELIGHTED THE VIENNESE**

👑 *For Franz Josef and Elisabeth above it was very much a love match. Neither of them had had a serious romantic interest before they met*

👑 *This portrait of the handsome, young Emperor below was painted in 1852, the year before he met Elisabeth*

Bildarchiv Preussischer Kulturbesitz

**T**HE FATEFUL MEETING BETWEEN FRANZ Josef and Elisabeth took place on 15 August 1853 at Ischl, a little summer resort much favoured by the imperial family. Sisi was aged 15 and Franz Josef was 22.

Strictly speaking it was not their first encounter, since both had been at another family gathering at Innsbruck in June 1848. Sisi had been a little girl of 10, and the 17-year-old Franz Josef, already an Archduke, had been too preoccupied with the revolutionary threat to think of falling in love.

Sisi had nevertheless found a Habsburg admirer in Franz Josef's 13-year-old brother, Karl Ludwig. He had continued to send her gifts year after year. He too was at Ischl, and may have entertained romantic hopes; but he was fated to be just a spectator of the romance that actually developed.

## Bewitched

One of the legends that grew up about the meeting was that Franz Josef first caught sight of Elisabeth in the woods. Dressed in white, with her long hair falling loosely over her shoulders, she appeared to him like some enchanted creature. Naturally, he fell in love with her at first sight.

The truth seems to have been less operatic, although just as romantic. Having arrived at the rendezvous, Ludovika and her daughters were immediately summoned to be presented to the Emperor. They were not given an opportunity to change out of their black travelling clothes, worn in mourning for a relative. The Archduchess sent her personal hairdresser in advance to make sure that Helene – but not Elisabeth – looked her best; and then the meeting was permitted to take place.

It seems to have been a relaxed family reunion, although there must have been many covert glances in the direction of the young Emperor, resplendent in his general's uniform. Franz Josef made non-commitally polite conversation with Helene, but one interested observer – his jealous younger brother Karl Ludwig – noticed how often the imperial gaze fell on Elisabeth, standing sweetly and modestly in the background with her governess.

## Elisabeth takes his eye

It was the same at dinner. Helene was given the place of honour, between Franz Josef and his father; but this made more obvious the Emperor's interest in the far end of the table, where Elisabeth, overwhelmed by shyness, sat tongue-tied in pretty confusion.

The court ball must have been an even

more intimidating experience, but it was a decisive event in the lives of Franz Josef and Elisabeth. She sat out the first dance, and it was her Aunt Sophie who made sure that the young girl would not be a wallflower by ordering one of the Emperor's aides to take her on to the floor.

Although she had never before partnered anyone but her dancing master, Elisabeth acquitted herself well in the polka – while Franz Josef stood watching, unable to take his eyes off her. When he had returned Elisabeth to her place, the aide whispered to a fellow officer, 'I think I've just danced with our future Empress.'

### Declaration of love

Nevertheless, as the evening went on the Emperor behaved as his rank demanded, paying courteous attention to his guests and dancing with both Bavarian Princesses. But when it was time for the Cotillion – the dance in which the choice of partner represented the ultimate compliment – it was Elisabeth whom Franz Josef led out on to the floor.

And when it was over, it was she to whom

*Bildarchiv Preussischer Kulturbesitz*

## 'Sisi is ascending the throne almost straight from the nursery'

### DUCHESS LUDOVIKA

he gave not only the cotillion bouquet but all the flowers that were customarily distributed among the ladies present. This was a remarkable breach of decorum on the part of a monarch who was a stickler for etiquette, and was consequently all the more striking as a spontaneous and passionate declaration of his love.

Now matters sped on to their inevitable conclusion. The Archduchess Sophie's attempts to resist proved useless. She pointed out that Elisabeth was little more than a child, unprepared for the responsibilities of adult life, let alone the weight of an imperial crown, whereas it was plain to see that Helene had the serious, dignified mien of a potential Empress. The normally dutiful Franz Josef was not to be moved, and he celebrated his 23rd birthday on 18 August by formally asking Ludovika for her daughter's hand.

### Engaged

Elisabeth's mother was evidently delighted by the prospect of becoming the Emperor's mother-in-law – even if his choice of bride

*Lami/V & A/Bridgeman*

came as something of a shock. She gave her consent without waiting for Duke Max's telegram of approval. Only when the prize had been secured did she succumb to motherly doubts, remarking worriedly that Sisi was 'ascending the throne almost straight from the nursery.'

The news travelled fast, and on the next day, Sunday 19 August, large crowds gathered to cheer the handsome young couple as they attended the local church. Franz Josef made the engagement official by asking for the priest's blessing on himself and his fiancée.

♛ *At 15, young Elisabeth* left *was beginning to blossom. Though her mother, intent on pressing Helene's claims to Franz Josef's hand, had paid little attention to her younger daughter's appearance before the meeting with the Emperor at Ischl, Elisabeth's artlessness and beauty shone through and captivated him*

♛ *The meeting at Ischl was essentially an informal family occasion* below, *though there was serious business afoot. There were few suitable options open to Archduchess Sophie in her role as marriage-broker to her son; this was her chance to find a bride from within her own family*

Usually so restrained and correct, the Emperor astonished his retinue by the passion with which he embraced Elisabeth. For her part, she too was swept away by her feelings. But whereas the Emperor's love, though powerful, was as straightforward as everything else about him, Elisabeth's complex, nervously intense nature reacted with a mixture of joy, embarrassment and trepidation to the strange new situation in which she found herself.

Along with the thrill of loving and being loved, she felt a sense of guilt at having unwittingly humiliated Helene, to whom she was deeply attached. She was upset, too, at all the stares and attention she was receiving, first from courtiers and later from the crowds of well-wishers who called out and threw flowers into the engaged couple's carriage. Since all this was another 'occupational hazard' of monarchy, Elisabeth's reaction did not bode well for the future.

## Joy and doubt

For the moment she was borne up by the romance of it all. When her mother brought her news of Franz Josef's offer and asked how she felt about him, Elisabeth blurted out, 'Of course I love him! How could anyone not love him!' Then she added, naively, 'But why, of all people, me?' The following day, as she began to realize the kind of life to which she had committed herself, Elisabeth told her governess, 'I do love him. But if only he were not an Emperor!' And she burst into tears. In the circumstances it seemed a natural reaction, touching but of no particular significance.

The days at Ischl fled past in a whirl of parties, balls and picnics, culminating in a grand lakeside fireworks' display in which the night sky was lit up by the lovers' entwined initials blazing beneath an imperial crown. Then, after a blissful late-August fortnight, the idyll was over. It was time to leave.

Kunsthistorisches Museum, Vienna

🖾 *After the engagement, the couple were able to spend some time together – though never alone – by driving out into the mountainous country around Ischl in a procession of landaus and carriages* above

## IMPERIAL HOLIDAY HOME

The Emperor Franz Josef and Elisabeth of Bavaria met and fell in love at Ischl, a little spa resort set among the lovely lakes and forests of Austria's Salzkammergut. The resort had been a family favourite since the time when the Emperor's mother, the Archduchess Sophie, had given birth to Franz Josef after taking the salt cure at Ischl to end her supposed barrenness. When her son married, the Archduchess presented him with the Kaiservilla, a house in the classical style which, suitably enlarged, became the imperial couple's summer home *below*. To Franz Josef, Ischl was 'the earthly paradise', and he returned every year to indulge his passion for hunting

Topham

Elisabeth and her family went back to their home in Bavaria, escorted as far as Salzburg by the Emperor. After a lingering farewell, he returned to the cares of state. A mountain of paperwork was waiting for him at the Hofburg, the Palace in Vienna from which he governed his empire of 40 million subjects. In the months before their marriage, which was planned for the following spring, the young couple could not hope to see a great deal of each other.

## Much to do

Over the next few months, both the Emperor and his bride-to-be were very busy indeed. Franz Josef was used to spending 10 hours a day with a pen in his hand. But the unsettling effects of romance led him to complain to his mother of 'this dreary desk-bound existence in which I am buried beneath state papers and beset by a hundred cares.' Mounting tensions in Europe added to his cares. Fortunately, though, when the situation erupted into the Crimean War, Franz Josef was able to keep Austria out of the conflict.

Among his paperwork were important documents relating to his marriage. The contract between the Emperor and his in-laws fixed the bride's dowry at 50,000 gulden. Franz Josef also calculated that 100,000 gulden would have to come out of the imperial budget to maintain Elisabeth and her household, and he even stipulated the pension she was to receive in the event of his death.

There was one absolutely inescapable formality – securing a dispensation from the Pope

Historisches Museum der Stadt, Vienna

👑 *The further link between the Royal houses of Austria and Bavaria represented by the engagement of Franz Josef and Elisabeth was marked by* souvenirs above *detailing the complex family trees of both families*

Lami/V & A/Bridgeman

👑 *In Austria, home of the waltz, the engagement was celebrated with lavish balls and parties* left. *The Habsburgs were long-term patrons of the Austrian musical tradition, maintaining many court musicians and court composers, such as Salieri and Gluck. Mozart, Haydn, Beethoven, Schubert and Strauss also lived and worked in Vienna*

♛ *Elisabeth's equestrian ability and grace in the saddle above helped endear her to Franz Josef, who commissioned this portrait of her, with Possenhofen in the background, at the time of their engagement. She was taught by her father, himself an accomplished horseman, and loved to accompany him on rides through the rugged countryside around Possenhofen*

♛ *On 20 April 1854 the 16-year-old Elisabeth, accompanied by her mother, left the Bavarian capital, Munich, for the three-day journey up the Danube to Vienna for her marriage right. Crowds lined the streets to wish her well*

for a marriage between first cousins. Evidently nobody dared to suggest that there were any dangers attached to yet another match involving two multiply inbred families, one of which – the Bavarian Wittlesbachs – was already producing an alarming number of wayward, abnormal peronalities.

## A stream of presents

Despite all Franz Josef's preoccupations, Sisi – as he had learned to call Elisabeth – was never far from his thoughts. At his desk he wrote to her almost every day. Courier after courier was

sent off to Bavaria with gifts of jewels, furs, a miniature of the Emperor in a diamond frame and even a parrot from the famous imperial zoo in Vienna.

Elisabeth may well have needed these attentions to keep her spirits up, for once back at her beloved home she seems to have suffered a reaction. At any rate she penned a little poem inspired by the migrating swallows. Its opening lines were:

*O swallows, lend me your wings so fleet*
*And bear me to far-off lands,*
*That I may rejoice in freedom sweet,*
*Released from my prisoner's bands.*

This longing for liberation is emphasized later in the poem, when Elisabeth is ready 'to forget the old love and the new' to experience the happiness of flight and freedom.

These were strange sentiments from a girl who was in love and was about to be married, even if the poem's air of romantic melancholy was something of a 19th-century cliché. If she was apprehensive about the constraints of life at court, a rebuke from her Aunt Sophie cannot have reassured her. In a letter, Sisi addressed the Archduchess – who was both her aunt and her prospective mother-in-law – as *Du* (the familiar form of 'you'), only to be told in no uncertain terms that even the Emperor never used anything but the formal *Sie* when addressing his mother.

## Lovers' meeting

In October, Franz Josef took the first opportunity to rush to Munich, covering the 400 kilometres (250 miles) in just 31 hours. When they met again the magic still worked. Seeing her at her most spontaneous and delightful, with her family around her at Possenhofen, the Emperor was more captivated than ever. On long rides through the forest he was delighted

to discover that his delicate, flower-like fiancée was confident and highly competent when she was on horseback.

She also bore up well under the strain of official festivities in Munich. Sisi was now someone of political importance, because she was strengthening the ties between Austria and Bavaria. She and Franz Josef attended the Munich Opera and the court ball, where her modestly correct behaviour and rapidly blossoming beauty made an indelible impression. The Emperor wrote enthusiastically to his mother, 'Every day I love Sisi more, and am more convinced that no one could be better suited to me.'

Franz Josef's visit acted as a tonic, and when he returned to Vienna, Elisabeth began to take her new role more seriously. It was not before time. 'I shall be the most ignorant Queen in Europe,' she had cried out in dismay, when she realized how few accomplishments she had mastered during her spasmodic studies. Now she applied herself to learning the history of 'her' empire and its peoples, and to mastering French and Italian.

## *'Every day I love Sisi more, and am more convinced that no one could be better suited to me'*

### FRANZ JOSEF

Elisabeth also had to endure sittings for portraits and to go through endless fittings for her trousseau. She was not yet deeply interested in clothes, and the wardrobe she would need amazed her: 31 dresses for formal occasions, 17 summer dresses, 168 undergarments, 240 pairs of gloves – the list was endless. As Elisabeth would learn, an Empress was never seen in even the most stunning creation on more than a handful of occasions, and lesser items were often worn only once.

### Romantic gestures

Franz Josef travelled to Bavaria again in December for Elisabeth's 16th birthday, and paid a final visit in March, just a month before the wedding. He brought with him the costliest gift so far: the famous set of diamonds and opals worn by the Archduchess Sophie at her own wedding. The Archduchess, disdainful of the slapdash habits of her relatives at Possenhofen, impressed on Franz Josef that he must per-

Historisches Museum der Stadt, Vienna

sonally make sure the gems were locked away.

At last the time came for Elisabeth to say farewell to Bavaria. On 20 April she left Munich for the Danube, where a steam-yacht waited to take her by river to her new home. Crowds lined the banks to watch the flower-strewn yacht as it made the first stage of the journey to Linz, where Elisabeth was to stay overnight.

And there, quite unexpectedly, was Franz Josef on the quayside. With romantic panache he had travelled nearly halfway from Vienna to welcome his bride as she set foot on Austrian soil, and to escort her to her lodgings. Next morning, at crack of dawn, he had to return to Vienna in time to head an official party that would meet Elisabeth at the end of her journey.

*When Elisabeth arrived at the port of Nussdorf above, huge crowds of Viennese were there to greet her, and to cheer their Emperor, who leapt aboard her boat before it had docked to embrace and kiss his fiancée*

*After spending the night of 22 April in the Schönbrunn palace, where she had her first taste of the restrictions of life in the Habsburg court, Elisabeth made a gala entry into Vienna on the eve of her wedding below*

Archiv Für Kunst & Geschichte

# A WARM WELCOME

The Emperor was not an imaginative young man, but he was inspired by love to perform these exquisitely ardent gestures. This was all the more remarkable as he was caught up in the European crisis caused by the outbreak of the Crimean War, and had just ordered troop mobilizations.

On 22 April, Elisabeth's yacht approached the little village of Nussdorf outside Vienna. Many thousands of people had left the capital to see their future Empress, and roars of approval went up when they sighted the little figure, dressed in a pink gown and bonnet waiting on the deck.

The Emperor stood on the landing stage with his parents, but boarded the ship before it had moored and kissed Elisabeth in front of everyone. Then a carriage transported her through cheering crowds to Schönbrunn, the Habsburg summer Palace situated on the outskirts of Vienna.

Interest in this Royal romance ran high abroad, and British readers were kept in touch by *The Times*. The newspaper's correspondent was struck by the charm of the occasion: 'The Princess Elisabeth smiled and bowed to her future subjects as if every face on which her eye rested belonged to an old and valued friend.

Some straight-laced critics would have preferred a more dignified and reserved deportment, but what has a young girl of 16, whose heart is overflowing with love and kindly feelings, to do with dignity and reserve?' *The Times* approved of the unreserved, very natural girl who was about to reign over the most etiquette-conscious and hidebound court in Europe.

## A fairy-tale procession

On 23 April, after a short drive from Schönbrunn to the traditional starting point, the Theresanium Palace, Elisabeth began her ceremonial entry into the capital. This was perhaps the most splendid public occasion of all, although Elisabeth is said to have been so tired of crowds and hand-kissings and tedious formalities that she dismissed the entire business as a circus freakshow. If so, it was one worthy of a fairy tale.

She rode in a glass coach with golden wheels and panels painted 150 years earlier by the great Flemish artist Peter Paul Rubens. Brilliantly liveried postillions helped to force a way through the good-tempered crowd, which cordons of Lancers had failed to hold in check. The city was *en fête*. All the public buildings were newly scrubbed, and flags, flowers and rosettes in blue and white, the Bavarian colours, were hanging everywhere.

The procession passed over a new bridge which had been named the Elisabeth Bridge,

*♛ The wedding of Franz Josef and Elisabeth took place right in the relatively modest confines of St Augustine's, the Hofburg parish church, which was lit by 10,000 candles for the glittering occasion. Elisabeth was escorted down the aisle by her mother and the Archduchess Sophie; the fathers of the bride and groom, though present, took no part in the ceremony*

*♛ Contemporary lithographs of the Royal couple show Elisabeth as a fresh-faced young girl left. Hand-coloured portraits such as this were sold in their thousands throughout Austria, and provided the people of the Habsburg Empire with their first image of the new Empress*

Franz Joseph,
Kaiser von Oeſtreich
geb. d.18 August 1830, beſtieg den Thron den 2. Decbr 1848.
vermählt d. 24. April 1854.

*Original u. Eigenthum No. 2816.*

Elisabeth,
Kaiſerin von Oeſtreich
geb: Herzogin von Baiern.

*Neu Ruppin zu haben bei Guſtav Kühn.*

and went on to its destination, the Hofburg. This was the huge Habsburg palace complex, whose thousands of rooms served as both imperial residence and centre of government.

## Glittering wedding

From the Hofburg, on the afternoon on 24 April 1854, Elisabeth of Bavaria set out to be married. The ceremony took place not in Vienna's famous St Stephen's Cathedral but, following tradition, in the Augustinerkirche, the parish church only a few yards down the street. Almost 1000 people squeezed into the church, their jewels, medals and orders gleaming and sparkling in the candle-light, enhancing the gilded splendours of the interior.

Elisabeth wore Sophie's diamond and opal diadem in her hair. Her white wedding dress was embroidered with gold and silver and decorated with blossoms. She was 'tall and graceful, with classic features and considerable poise, although still quite a young girl.' Despite the grandeur of the occasion she did not falter.

Franz Josef, still only 23 but used to both the glitter and the tedium of ceremonial, made his vows in a loud, firm voice and remained attentive during the sermon delivered by the long-winded Archbishop of Vienna. When the young couple exchanged rings, a salvo of guns and peals of church bells throughout the city informed the populace that Austria had a new Empress.

## Traditional ceremonies

The procesion forced its way back along the narrow street, amid fanfares and cheers, to the Hofburg. There, the traditional 'hand kissing' ritual had to be gone through. The Emperor and Empress sat on their thrones in the great ceremonial hall while a never-ending queue of Austrian dignitaries filed past. Each of them

planted a kiss on the Empress's right hand which – a nice practical note – was permitted to rest on a cushion.

After the formal banquet that followed, the young couple were allowed to retire for the night, although only in approved ceremonial fashion. Her way lit by 12 pages with golden candelabra, the bride was conducted to her bedchamber by her mother, who undressed her and put her to bed.

Then, after a discreet interval, Franz Josef arrived, accompanied by his mother. Worn out with polite small talk and volumes of good advice from the Archduchess, Elisabeth pretended to be asleep until her mother-in-law had departed, leaving husband and wife alone together for the first time.

♛ *The platitudinous sermon of the Archbishop prolonged the wedding ceremony to the early evening, when Franz Josef took his new bride back to the Hofburg's throne-room to accept the homage of members of the Austrian aristocracy left. Two hours of this so exhausted the teenage Empress that she ate nothing at the family banquet which followed*

# SCHÖNBRUNN

*The Palace of Schönbrunn is in the western suburbs of Vienna. It was built at the end of the 17th century, on the site of a palace razed by marauding Turks in 1683. House and gardens were remodelled in 1749 at the orders of Maria Theresa, Empress of Austria from 1740 to 1780, and her homely, bourgeois influence still moderates the grandeur of the 1,441-room palace*

Bavaria-Verlag

Tony Stone Worldwide

♛ The taste for Chinoiserie spread through Europe in the 18th century, but the Habsburg Empire had little direct trade with the East, and the oval 'Chinese Room' in the Palace *above* is distinguished only by its Oriental urns and lacquer-panelled walls

♛ The wonderful formal gardens of the Schönbrunn Palace, with their many lakes, ponds and fountains *right*, set off the yellow facade and have given the Palace both its name (literally 'beautiful fountain') and nickname, 'the Versailles of Vienna'

Bavaria-Verlag

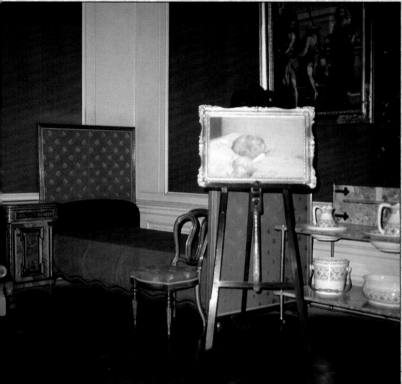

♔ The decor of Maria Theresa's study *left* typifies the opulence of Schönbrunn's public rooms. The Empress's gilded rococo desk sits below a portrait of her father, Charles VI, while the light from the crystal chandeliers spills on to gilt-rimmed lacquer panels and a magnificent inlaid wooden floor. Other rooms *right* have tapestries rather than gilding and panelling covering the walls, and continue the 18th-century theme with heavy, baroque, cabriole-legged furniture. Perhaps the finest room in the whole palace is the Great Gallery at the front of the building. Its ceilings are covered with fresco panels by Gregorio Guglielmi which celebrate Austrian military, artistic and scientific triumphs *above right*. In stark contrast is the room *above* which the ascetic Franz Josef used as his sleeping-quarters all his life. The portrait on the easel is of the Emperor on his death-bed

# UNHAPPY ELISABETH

**YOUNG AND HIGHLY STRUNG, ELISABETH FOUND IT HARD TO ADAPT TO LIFE AT THE IMPERIAL COURT. SHE WAS SOON IN CONFLICT WITH HER INTERFERING MOTHER-IN-LAW**

♛ *In 1854, shortly after their marriage, Sisi and Franz Josef below stroll on a terrace in the grounds of Schönbrunn Palace. Although Sisi looked remarkably mature for a 16 year-old, she was still little more than a girl emotionally, and was lacking in self-confidence*

AT THE HABSBURG COURT, THE STRESSES OF an imperial wedding were not alleviated by the prospect of a relaxed, private honeymoon. Instead, the wedding night was followed by a taxing round of duties. There were receptions to be held and deputations to be received.

The dignitaries who came from the various parts of Franz Josef's multi-ethnic Empire had to be met by an imperial couple attired in the appropriate national costume. The costume changes – which might have thrilled a more clothes-conscious girl – simply exasperated Elisabeth. Only the Hungarian magnates, in their magnificent, almost oriental garb, aroused much enthusiasm in her.

Two days after the wedding, the event was celebrated again, this time by a great Court ball in the Hofburg to which 2000 people were invited. The orchestra was conducted by the 'Waltz King', Johann Strauss the Younger. Elisabeth presided with the imperial crown on her head – a crown which, with ominous symbolism, she found almost too heavy to bear, and which gave her a terrible headache.

However, there were lighter moments, notably an equestrian performance in Vienna's great public pleasure-ground, the Prater. The

> ## *World affairs don't come to a stop during a honeymoon'*
>
> FRANZ JOSEF

imperial party enjoyed this in an atmosphere of relative informality, with all aristocratic and fashionable Vienna thronging around them.

Despite its great size, and the care taken by the Archduchess Sophie to redecorate it, the Hofburg was a gloomy place where Court etiquette was at its most oppressive. At the end of April, after Elisabeth's family had returned to Bavaria, Franz Josef took her to Laxenburg, a small Palace (by Habsburg standards) in the countryside not far from Vienna.

## Work comes first

Here, if she had not realized it before, Elisabeth must have understood just what it meant to be an Empress. The 'honeymoon' was confined to

the evenings. Early each morning, Franz Josef left Laxenburg for the capital; and when Elisabeth remonstrated, he told her without mincing words that 'World affairs don't come to a stop during a honeymoon.' Admittedly the Crimean War had created an international situation that had to be carefully monitored; but, as Elisabeth would find out, in good times and bad the Emperor's routine varied very little – he was a workaholic.

The fact was that Franz Josef, at 23, was already set in his ways and would never change, although he lived for another 63 years. He was chained to his desk – or rather he chained himself to it – because he insisted on reading and personally annotating every state document of any significance.

Incapable of delegating responsibility or sharing authority – even with his own kin – he condemned himself to a bureaucratic treadmill which left him little time for personal relationships. He was capable of suffering when afflicted by family tragedies, but he was first and foremost an institution rather than a man.

This was less obvious while Franz Josef was young, ardent and handsome, although Elisabeth felt the effects of his chosen life-style from the beginning. In these early days the Emperor himself sensed nothing wrong: he gave Sisi everything she wanted, and he himself was 'as much in love as a lieutenant and as happy as a god.'

## Sisi's melancholy

At Laxenburg Elisabeth was again writing melancholy poems. The feelings she expressed were unexpected ones from a bride of a few weeks:

> Oh, would that I'd never abandoned
> The road that meant freedom for me,
> And taken instead that broader way
> Down the path of vanity.

The cause of Elisabeth's melancholy was not simply Franz Josef's absences. She hated the Court world of stifling constraints and formalities and felt temperamentally ill-equipped to cope. And she already had an enemy: the Archduchess Sophie, who for Sisi embodied everything oppressive and hateful at the Habsburg Court.

## Dominating Archduchess

There seemed no getting away from the domineering Archduchess. Elisabeth's apartments in the Hofburg and at Schönbrunn had been decorated and furnished according to Sophie's taste. All the Empress's staff and servants were the Archduchess's nominees and owed their first loyalty to her.

Elisabeth had had a foretaste of the future on her arrival at Schönbrunn. She had been met

*Bildarchiv Preussischer Kulturbesitz*

by a grim-featured chief lady-in-waiting, the 56-year-old Countess Esterhazy-Liechtenstein, who had lost no time in instructing her to get by heart a heavy tome describing the correct ceremonial procedures for her state entry to Vienna. One of the Emperor's aides commented that the Countess 'treated the young Empress in the manner of a governess.'

Perhaps this was natural, if insensitive, in view of Elisabeth's age. Sophie certainly felt she was being benevolent in guiding, instructing and correcting her 16-year-old daughter-in-law. After all, the Empress's duties and Court etiquette had to be learned, and it was better done in private than in public.

🕊 *An aquatint from the first half of the 19th century* above, *showing St Michael's Square in central Vienna. In the background is the Hofburg Palace, the large, gloomy building that became Elisabeth's Viennese home*

👑 *Vienna was the musical capital of Europe in the middle of the 19th century, famed for its waltzes composed by the Strauss family. Open-air concerts and balls* below *were a regular feature of summer life in the Austrian capital*

Archiv Fur Kunst & Geschichte

👑 *Franz Josef and Elisabeth right soon after their wedding, depicted against the backdrop of the fountain in the gardens of the Schönbrunn Palace, outside Vienna. They made a handsome couple and in these early days had the love and support of the Austrian people*

👑 *Franz Josef and Sisi spent their honeymoon on the imperial estate at Laxenburg, a few miles south of Vienna. They lived there in Franzensburg, the early 19th century Gothic castle* below, *which had been built on the lake by Franz I. The Laxenburg estate was once the favourite retreat of an earlier ruler, Empress Maria Theresa, who filled the grounds with temples, statuary and cascades, as well as installing a theatre and skittle alley in another castle in the park*

However, Sophie's righteous severity seems to have masked an unconscious jealousy of Elisabeth. The unromantic nature of Sophie's own marriage probably made her insensitive to any marital considerations except the interests of the dynasty.

At any rate she upset Elisabeth, and possibly alienated her for ever, immediately after the wedding night. She insisted that the young couple join her for breakfast, and throughout the meal made a series of pointed enquiries about the success of the night's proceedings!

Even at Laxenburg the implacable Sophie descended all too frequently, telling her cornered niece that a whole range of activities, from failing to wear gloves to drinking a glass of beer, were 'unsuitable', or 'improper', or simply 'not done'. Poor Elisabeth discovered that, although she had the title of Empress, she was in reality little more than a privileged marionette. A girl of 16, surrounded by strangers, Elisabeth had neither the strength of character nor the experience to assert herself.

## Outbursts

Occasionally Sisi burst out in front of her retinue with some indiscreet remark that was faithfully reported back to the Archduchess. As time went on Sisi began to complain to Franz Josef about the Archduchess's interference, but he refused to intervene between his mother and his wife. Assuring Elisabeth that Sophie did everything for the best, he would just retreat behind his state papers. The Archduchess herself maintained a freezingly correct attitude, rarely criticizing Elisabeth to others except to remark that it was a shame that Sisi was such a nervy little thing.

Elisabeth adjusted as well as she could, and there were still happy times during the first months, especially when the Emperor and Empress left behind Habsburg Vienna — and Archduchess Sophie — to make a summer tour of Franz Josef's Bohemian domains. Elisabeth played her part to perfection on the state occasions, enjoying the change of scenery and the sense of release that travelling brought her.

## Unhappy pregnancy

It was over all too soon, and the last glimmer of freedom disappeared once Elisabeth discovered that she was pregnant. The Archduchess was put in charge of her, and she was subjected to a regime of kindly but claustrophobic atten-

Roger-Viollet

tion that made her feel like a brood mare subject to public scrutiny. Even her most harmless amusements were censured, and the Archduchess revealed a superstitious streak when she wrote to Franz Josef: 'I do not think Sisi should concern herself so much with her parrots, for if a woman is always looking at animals, especially during the early months, her children are likely to resemble them. She would be better employed looking in her mirror, or at you. I should be well pleased with that kind of looking.'

Pregnancy did not agree with Elisabeth, whose fits of sickness and depression reflected her disgust with her changing shape. Disillusioned by reality, she was already retreating into herself and beginning to make a cult of her own beauty as something to be maintained in ideal form.

She seems to have used her condition as an excuse to avoid sexual relations with Franz Josef. Although she loved him, she probably never found the physical side of marriage much to her taste. The strain on the Emperor, although he appeared as stoical as ever, must have been considerable.

### A daughter

On 5 March 1855, after a relatively short and easy labour, Elisabeth gave birth to a girl whom it was decided would be named Sophie. Sisi's views on the matter were apparently not consulted. The baby's gender was something of a disappointment, since it was desirable for dynastic reasons that Elisabeth should produce a direct male heir. So as she wearily remarked,

♛ *An early photographic portrait of Elisabeth, by the Austrian photographic pioneer, Franz Hanfstaengel top. The picture, taken in the late 1850s, captures Elisabeth at the height of her beauty. In her left hand she holds her private journal. She confided her intimate thoughts to this and, throughout her life, she would often write poetry inset in her journal. Not all her poems were melancholic. In later life, as she grew in confidence, she developed quite a talent for satirical poetry*

## STRONG-MINDED ARCHDUCHESS

Franz Josef's strong-minded mother, the Archduchess Sophie, did much to shape the Emperor's character and destiny, both personal and political. Born in 1805, the daughter of King Maximilian I of Bavaria, Sophie was married at 19 to the mediocre Austrian Archduke Franz Karl, by whom she had four sons. When revolution engulfed Austria in 1848, she was one of the few people at the Habsburg Court who kept her head. One admirer remarked that she had 'the finest political head among the members of the Royal Family.' It was largely thanks to Sophie that Franz Josef became Emperor, but her rigid ideas about imperial etiquette and child-rearing made her relations with the Empress Elisabeth difficult. She lived to see her second son, Ferdinand Maximillian, shot by Mexican revolutionaries, but died in 1872, before even more family tragedies struck the Habsburgs

Winterhalter/Marianne Haller

*♛ Elisabeth's tall, slim figure, her pale complexion and her long, glossy auburn tresses were depicted to advantage by many portrait painters. This one above is by Franz Xaver Winterhalter. The shy, restless teenager who, during her engagement, had found sitting for artists such a trial, nevertheless became an ideal model for painters. As Sisi became more aware of her own beauty, sittings became more pleasurable, both for her and the artist. She soon began to take pride in the paintings which would immortalize her good looks*

she 'would have to go through the whole dreary business again.'

A battery of nurses and other attendants had already been chosen – by Sophie – to look after the infant, whose nursery was situated on the same floor as the Archduchess's apartments. It was Elisabeth who had to toil upstairs to visit her child. This state of affairs was only remedied after the birth of a second daughter, named Gisela, on 15 July 1856. Franz Josef was persuaded to have the nursery transferred to an apartment close to the Empress, despite the protests of the Archduchess.

In the heat of the moment Sophie said Elisabeth was more interested in her horses than in her children; and there was some truth in the accusation. Apart from using them in her struggle with the Archduchess, Elisabeth had only limited time for her girls – although the same might have been said of most aristocratic European mothers of the period.

This was Elisabeth's first small victory over the Archduchess, and a clear signal that she was beginning to grow up and could hold her own. Franz Josef, as much in love with her as ever, was finding it increasingly difficulty to ignore her wishes.

## Legendary beauty

One good reason was that Elisabeth's beauty was now coming to its astonishing early maturity, apparently unaffected by two pregnancies. The lines of her face grew firmer, setting off the wonderful complexion, straight, dark eyebrows and lustrous, deep-set eyes. Her low voice and mysterious smile were partly natural and partly acquired to conceal her one serious defect, the discoloured teeth that were probably a genetic inheritance.

Her tall, graceful figure showed to advantage in the voluminous fashionable crinolines that made smaller women look dumpy. But the Empress's crowning glory was her long, glossy, auburn hair, which became the centre of a daily ritual that included conditioning with quantities of eggs and brandy.

To say that Elisabeth was beautiful had by now ceased to be the kind of empty compliment that was automatically paid to royalty. Her loveliness was becoming a European legend – so much so that Franz Josef or his advisers realized that it might have a political value, softening and glamorizing the image of the monarchy. With this in mind, in the winter

of 1856-57, Franz Josef took Elisabeth with him for an extended state visit to Venice and Milan.

The Emperor's Italian subjects detested Austrian rule and hoped one day to become part of a united Italy. Nothing was likely to change their views, but the visit did achieve a limited success. As the British consul reported, even Italians who had nothing but hostile silence to offer the Emperor and Empress, crowded the city streets to see the celebrated beauty of Elisabeth.

## Mutual fascination

In the summer of 1857, the experiment was repeated when Franz Josef and Elisabeth visited Hungary, where memories of the 1848 revolution and its bloody suppression were still fresh. But there was a wide vein of romantic gallantry in the Hungarians, and they responded enthusiastically to a Queen who was both ravishingly beautiful and a superb horsewoman.

Elisabeth herself was thrilled by these daredevil horsemen, with their elaborate costumes, leopardskins and high-plumed shakos. They had made a considerable impression on her much earlier, when she received a Hungarian deputation after her wedding, as her Aunt Sophie had acidly noted. The Archduchess detested the Hungarians because they were the Emperor's most discontented and dangerous subjects. Her dislike was perhaps another reason for Elisabeth to take the opposite attitude and, in time, she would become an ardent champion of Hungarian rights.

The visit was to be tragically cut short. Despite the Archduchess's opposition, Elisabeth had insisted on taking the children with her, although little Sophie was known to be a frail and sickly child. In Budapest she became sufficiently ill to cause alarm, and her parents were summoned to her bedside.

### Shattering death

On 31 May, after an agonizing 12 hours in which Franz Josef and Elisabeth watched the little girl grow weaker from fever and spitting blood, Sophie died. The cause of the death was unknown, but it may have been typhoid.

Franz Josef telegraphed the news to his parents. 'Our little one is an angel in heaven. We are utterly crushed. Sisi is resigned to the will of heaven.' But in reality it was Franz Josef who was resigned. In such situations — and there were to be many in his life — his ability to carry on with his official duties stood him in good stead.

Elisabeth was overwhelmed with grief and guilt, blaming herself for bringing the child to Hungary, and also for leaving her behind in Budapest while she toured with Franz Josef. It was almost a day before exhaustion weakened her resistance and she allowed herself to be led away from the body of her child. For months afterwards she led a nearly solitary existence, taking lonely walks and rides, and scarcely speaking to anyone but her husband.

*♛ Franz Josef and his advisers soon realized that Elisabeth's beauty was a positive advantage to the Austrian throne. Her attractiveness and natural charm captivated many who might otherwise have been antagonistic. Sisi would often accompany Franz Josef on official visits to outlying provinces. They are seen* left *on a visit to the mining town of Loeben, which went to great lengths to provide a warm welcome for the imperial couple*

*♛ Empress Elisabeth below in 1855 after the birth of her first child, Sophie. Though just 17, Elisabeth was becoming more poised all the time as she grew into her roles as wife, mother and Empress*

# BIRTH OF A SON AND HEIR

Something like normality returned at the end of the year, when Elisabeth discovered that she was pregnant again. The anxious months passed until 21 August 1858, when she went into labour at Schönbrunn. This time the birth pangs were protracted and severe, and the Palace rang with Elisabeth's screams. But when it was over, a jubilant Franz Josef was able to tell her that she had been delivered of a healthy boy who would carry on the Habsburg name.

The tiny infant came into the world with a pomp that seemed to augur a glittering destiny. He was Rudolf, Crown Prince of the Austrian Empire, and as he lay bawling in his golden cradle his father made him a member of the Order of the Golden Fleece. Outside, 101 guns thundered to let the capital know that the ancient House of Habsburg had an heir.

*Hulton Picture Company*

⚜ *An etching of Empress Elisabeth* left, *wearing a wreath of ivy leaves and a spray of ivy at her breast. Although still in her teens, Elisabeth's beauty was becoming a European legend*

## *'I can't tell you how much I love you and how much I think about you'*

### FRANZ JOSEF TO SISI

As their joyful, loving behaviour demonstrated, Franz Josef and Elisabeth still cared for each other, despite all the strains put upon their marriage. However, a new and serious problem arose when the Archduchess Sophie was put in charge of the Crown Prince's upbringing. Franz Josef replied to Elisabeth's protests with an infuriating, unanswerable question: who was better fitted for the task than the mother who had brought him up?

The decision cannot have done much for Elisabeth's self-confidence, especially after the death of little Sophie, when her nervous fears led her to believe that people were saying that she was not fit to be a mother. And it was hardly the way to make her take seriously the responsibilities she already found irksome.

### Italian campaign
In his characteristically obtuse fashion, Franz Josef tended to dismiss the now deep-seated antagonism between his mother and his wife as 'trivial women's disputes'. This attitude became a little more understandable in the spring of 1859, as the Emperor found himself drawn

into a war with Italy which involved Austria in one catastrophe after another. After a time, Franz Josef himself took command, only to suffer humiliating defeats in battle and, later, at the conference table.

The letters he and Elisabeth exchanged during the campaign reveal a great deal about both of them. 'I can't tell you how much I love you and how much I think about you', he wrote. She must take care of her precious health and keep more regular hours. She must stop going out alone with Holmes, her English riding instructor: it was improper. And surely she could respond to the crisis: 'My dear, dear angel: I beg of you, for the love you have vowed to me, take hold of yourself. Show yourself in the city from time to time, and visit public in-

⚜ *Emperor Franz Josef and Empress Elisabeth riding out together* below. *Both were fine riders. For Elisabeth, horses had been a passion since her childhood at Possenhofen. In Austria, where good horsemanship was highly valued, she had plenty of opportunities to show her skills, both in the indoor dressage arena at the Hofburg in Vienna and in the extensive grounds of the imperial residences*

*Historisches Museum der Stadt, Vienna*

Archiv Fur Kunst & Geschichte

stitutions. You have no idea how much of a help this would be to me . . .'

Elisabeth's first impulse was an unrealistic one. She wanted to join her husband at army headquarters. When he explained that this was impossible, she expressed her fears for his safety, and her love for him, in her rather self-regarding fashion: 'What shall I do without you? Have you forgotten me in the midst of all these events? Do you love me still?'

### Elisabeth's contribution

When she realized the gravity of the situation she showed that she could rise to an emergency. A military hospital was set up at Laxenburg, and Elisabeth's efforts to cheer and help the wounded were all the more effective because she violated protocol by making personal contact with the men. In any other circumstances this would have earned her a sharp rebuke from the Emperor or her aunt.

Franz Josef returned to a war-weary, demoralized Vienna which gave him an icy reception. His public appearances were infrequent, and he spent long periods at Laxenburg with his family. Here, however, there was little peace, since his wife and his mother were on more acrimonious terms than ever.

♛ *Franz Josef and Elisabeth in 1859* above *with Crown Prince Rudolf, on Elisabeth's lap, and Princess Gisela. Elisabeth, devasted and reclusive after the tragic death of her eldest daughter, returned to a semblance of normality after the birth of Crown Prince Rudolf, the longed-for heir to the Habsburg throne*

## A PASSION FOR HUNTING

In England, the 19th century was the golden age of fox-hunting, which was celebrated in a multitude of colourful prints *below* and in stories such as Surtees' *Jorrock's Jaunts and Jollities*. As a pursuit it was quintessentially English. When the Emperor Franz Josef followed the hounds at Gödollo, in Hungary, he wore the pink jacket prescribed by the Royal Hunt and adhered to its code. His Empress, who often rode with her husband and later with the Pytchley and other famous hunts, was hailed by English huntsmen as 'the Queen of the Chase'

E.B Herbet/Gavin Graham Gallery/Bridgeman

# A LEGENDARY BEAUTY

*The Empress Eugénie of France described Elisabeth of Austria as 'the loveliest crowned head in Europe' and Elisabeth, well aware of her dazzling beauty, chose clothes to show it to perfection. Cream and white were among her favourite colours since they complemented her glowing auburn hair, and her garments were always tight-fitting to show her slender figure*

♛ This simple crinoline day dress in spotted organdie *right* was worn by the Empress soon after her marriage in 1854. Elisabeth's slender figure, which in later years she took great pains to retain, is shown off by the fitted bodice and tiny waist

♛ Elisabeth, her auburn hair characteristically braided *below*, wears a short Hungarian-style, fringed and embroidered cape over a fitted gown with billowing crinoline skirt

*Dress decorated with elaborate stitching on neckline, sleeves and bodice*

*Silk braid trim sewn into a scallop pattern*

*Circular, crinoline skirt, worn over a hooped petticoat*

Lynne Robinson

Interfoto

👑 Elisabeth, a fine horsewoman, in the top hat, tailored bodice and full skirt typical of the riding habit *left*

👑 The Empress Elisabeth's décolleté evening gown in flame-coloured shot silk *below* sports a fashionable white lace 'bertha', along with lace sleeves and flounces

Décolleté neckline, typical of fashionable evening wear

Gown worn with a velvet choker encrusted with jewels, bracelet-length evening gloves, trimmed with bracelets and hair circlet and brooches all of gold, diamonds and rubies

Evening gown encrusted with jewels and embroidery in a floral design

Ermine trim on shoulders, 'apron' skirt and train

👑 Empress Elisabeth wore this jewel-encrusted gown *left* to the grand reception to celebrate her silver wedding anniversary in 1879 at the Hofburg Palace in Vienna

# RESTLESS YEARS

**THE MARRIAGE HIT A TROUBLED TIME, AFFECTING ELISABETH PHYSICALLY AND MENTALLY. SHE FOUND RELIEF IN LONG TRIPS ABROAD AND ALSO TOOK UP THE MAGYAR CAUSE AND FOX-HUNTING WITH GUSTO**

T HERE SEEMS TO HAVE BEEN NO ADVANCE warning of the first major crisis in the Emperor's marriage. This broke in October 1860, when Elisabeth resolutely declared that she was ill and needed to winter abroad.

She was certainly not very well, but doctors were unable to find a reason for her sore throats, coughs and other ailments. The main physical cause was probably her run-down condition caused by dieting, which she pursued obsessively to the point of anorexia. The more important mental cause was a nervous depression so severe that the only refuge she could find was in flight. No Austrian or European spa would do. She chose Madeira — somewhere as far away as was possible.

## *Unfaithful*

Rumours current at the time hint at the real cause of the crisis. Elisabeth was thought to have discovered that Franz Josef had been unfaithful to her — some said with a Polish lady he had known before his marriage. It would not have been surprising if the Emperor had sought more accommodating and less demanding company than his adored, but sexually cold and endlessly difficult, wife. To Elisabeth, however, beleaguered at Court but at least seemingly secure within the fortress of her beauty, Franz Josef's betrayal must have come as a crushing blow.

And, the rumours suggest, there was worse to come. Worried by mysterious swellings of her wrist and knee joints, Elisabeth visited a doctor incognito and was told that she had a sexual infection, which could only have been transmitted to her by Franz Josef. This was terribly shocking by any normal 19th-century standards, and must have been devastating for a woman like Elisabeth, with her overdeveloped distaste for physical realities.

If this episode really occurred it would

Winterhalter/Marianne Haller

👑 *This portrait of Franz Josef in the uniform of a Grand Marshal of the Austrian army* **left** *was executed by Winterhalter in 1865*

👑 *Elisabeth* **right** *on her first visit to Corfu. She so liked the island that she returned to it frequently, eventually building the neo-classical Achilleion Palace* **below** *as her residence there*

👑 *Elisabeth developed a strong bond with her eccentric cousin, King Ludwig of Bavaria* **above**. *She regarded him as a soul spirit, as misunderstood by ordinary people as herself*

👑 *This Winterhalter portrait of Elisabeth, with silver stars decorating her hair and gown* **left**, *captures her ethereal beauty*

> **'I am longing to see my darling Sisi again after such a long separation'**
>
> FRANZ JOSEF

explain Franz Josef's extraordinary tolerance – born of guilt – for Elisabeth's whims and the reckless extravagances in which she later indulged.

Whatever the exact truth, she got her way. To keep up appearances it was announced that the Empress was suffering from an infection of the lungs, a chillingly convincing phrase in an age when tuberculosis was a deadly disease.

### Travel acts as a tonic

A sympathetic Queen Victoria of England lent the Empress her ocean-going yacht, and Franz Josef escorted his wife on her journey as far as Bamberg in Bavaria. After their leave-taking, she and her party travelled to Antwerp, and from there by yacht to Madeira.

On the voyage to Madeira, everybody but Elisabeth was seasick, and her health improved dramatically in spite of the rough weather. Much of her ill-health was clearly brought on by misery and boredom, vanishing – for a time – as soon as she had a change of scene. Sunny, exotic Madeira began by delighting Elisabeth and ended by boring her.

The Hofburg had a worse effect on her spirits, and soon after her return to Vienna in the spring of 1862, she was so ill that she was widely believed to be dying. She took flight again, this time to Corfu, with which she had fallen in love on her leisurely voyage back from Madeira. Again she made a miraculous recovery on shipboard, and after a long summer on the island she was difficult to entice back, although Franz Josef wrote pathetically that 'I am longing to see my darling Sisi again after such a long separation.'

Elisabeth did go back, but very much on her own terms. Marital relations were not resumed, and the Empress would attend only the minimum of State receptions. Each year she would visit an Austrian spa, Bad Kissingen, and her annual trip to see her family at Possenhofen provided an important emotional release.

### Family problems

Most of Elisabeth's brothers and sisters were now married, and there were already signs that she was not the only member of the family afflicted with the wayward Wittelsbach temperament. At Bad Kissingen she saw much of her cousin, the handsome, eccentric, homosexual King Ludwig II of Bavaria, who was devoted to her. They saw themselves as poetic souls, at odds with a brutal reality, and developed a strong bond.

Back in Vienna, Elisabeth's sister, Maria Sophia, the ex-Queen of Naples who had lost her throne during the upheavals in Italy, arrived in an advanced state of pregnancy by a young man who was not her husband. It says much for Elisabeth's growing confidence that she was able to make efficient arrangements for delivering the child in complete privacy.

A further sign of confidence was the ultimatum she delivered Franz Josef in the summer of 1865. She put it in writing, so that there should be not mistake about it – or perhaps because she felt Franz Josef could only give serious attention to a matter if it arrived on his desk in a document. Elisabeth demanded full control of her personal affairs, including her place of residence, the dismissal of Rudolf's tutor, and sole power to direct her children's upbringing. Faced with the threat of her final departure, Franz Josef capitulated.

This was less of a victory over the Archduchess than it might once have been, since Franz Josef, still obsessed with the army, had handed Rudolf over to a harsh military man whose severe régime, designed to harden his pupil, only succeeded in making him nervous and distraught. Having once gained her point, Elisabeth did not take a particularly close interest in her children's upbringing, but she had achieved a good deal in giving Rudolf the chance of a more normal boyhood.

At 27 Elisabeth was more beautiful than ever, still adored by her husband, and at last her own mistress. But if she had ever had the capacity for sustained happiness, it had long ago vanished. She was as restless as ever, easily upset when away but still more depressed at having to return to Vienna: 'I can't say I enjoy the

Popperfoto

♛ *Of the Habsburg brothers, only Franz Josef (seated)* above *seemed relatively normal. Archduke Karl Ludwig* left *became a religious fanatic; the headstrong, stubborn Maximilian, Emperor of Mexico, died before a firing squad; and Archduke Ludwig Victor led a wasted life as a frivolous, mischief-making homosexual*

prospect of coming home, for I'm appalled by the thought of all the boring moments which await me in the family circle.'

Elisabeth wrote this to one of her few confidantes, Ida Ferenczy, a Hungarian. The Empress's interest in Hungary had grown stronger with the years. She learned to speak the language fluently, and went so far as to speak Hungarian with her intimates in public, deliberately excluding the ladies-in-waiting and Court officials, whom she still believed to be her enemies.

## Hungarian champion

Her mastery of Hungarian proved useful when she and Franz Josef visited the country. The irresistible combination of Elisabeth's beauty and her known sympathy with Magyar grievances completely won over her hosts. Even Franz Josef, who had once remarked dismissively that she only liked the Hungarians because they were picturesque, now admitted that here, at least, 'Sisi is a great help to me'. But her pleas that he should conciliate his proud, troublesome subjects fell on deaf ears.

This changed rapidly after a new and even more disastrous war broke out. With the Austrian armies collapsing under the weight of a Prussian onslaught, it seemed at one point as though Vienna — and the Habsburg dynasty itself — might fall. Once more Elisabeth assumed a helpful public role, even steeling herself to assist at an amputation when the wounded man requested it.

As the crisis deepened, Franz Josef entrusted Elisabeth with a mission of real importance: to retain the fragile loyalty of the Hungarians by capitalizing on their passionate

## HUNGARIAN FRIENDS

Believing herself surrounded by enemies at the Austrian Court, the Empress Elisabeth chose Hungarians – outsiders like herself – as her intimate friends and confidantes. The first of these was Ida Ferenczy *right*, a country girl whom Elisabeth is supposed to have selected as the only untitled person on a list of possible helpers. Ida had close contacts with Hungarian nationalists, notably the handsome, magnetic Count Julius Andrassy. Elisabeth was to promote his career so ardently that court gossip would declare they were lovers. Elisabeth demanded the exclusive devotion of those she favoured, and made sure that neither Ida Ferenczy nor a later, more aristocratic friend, Marie Festetics, were able to marry

Bildarchiv Preussischer Kulturbesitz

Marianne Haller

Interfoto

'*I must . . . continue to bear patiently the lonely existence to which I have long been accustomed*'

FRANZ JOSEF

admiration of her. In this she was outstandingly successful. The Emperor's only complaint was that, once installed in Budapest, she proved reluctant to leave.

The war had effected a reconciliation between them, and they were again living as man and wife. But Franz Josef soon realized that Elisabeth remained as restless as ever: 'I must simply make the best of it and continue to bear patiently the lonely existence to which I have long been accustomed.'

## Magyar monarchs

Paradoxically, Austria's defeat accomplished everything that Elisabeth had wanted for such a long time. To preserve the shaken state, the whole basis of the Empire was changed, and Elisabeth's beloved Hungarians were admitted as full partners in what now became known as the Dual Monarchy of Austria-Hungary.

On 8 June 1867, Franz Josef and Elisabeth took part in a second coronation before the altar of Budapest Cathedral. Amid scenes of splendid pageantry and popular acclaim, they were annointed and crowned King and Queen of Hungary. In Hungarian eyes, Elisabeth was the heroine of the hour, looking ravishing in coronation robes designed by the Parisian couturier Worth.

Franz Josef also had his moment of glory. Still wearing his robes and crown, as custom prescribed, he rode to the top of a hill and, without dismounting, indicated the four points of the compass with drawn sword and swore to defend Hungary's frontiers. For a moment, with regal bearing and flawless horsemanship, he seemed once more like the romantic hero who had once swept Elisabeth off her feet.

*The Coronation of Elisabeth and Franz Josef as King and Queen of Hungary above was a glittering occasion which marked the height of their popularity. Eyewitnesses, including the composer Franz Liszt, confirm that Elisabeth looked divinely beautiful. Her Coronation robes inset were created by Worth, the famous Parisian couturier, who had adapted the Hungarian national costume in a skirt and train of white and silver brocade embroidered in jewels, with a black velvet bodice laced in pearls*

37

The Royal couple's euphoria was clouded by the news that the Emperor's brother, Maximilian, who had unwisely accepted the Mexican throne, had been shot by rebels. This was the first of a series of Habsburg and Wittelsbach tragedies that were to darken Franz Josef's and Elisabeth's lives. In this case the Emperor's habitual stoicism made it hard to know whether he was much affected, since there was little love lost between him and Maximilian.

### Beloved daughter

The fruit of Elisabeth's reconciliation with Franz Josef was a daughter, Valerie, born in Budapest on 22 April 1868. Elisabeth felt for her fourth child the mother-love so conspicuously absent in her relations with Gisela and Rudolf. And, as always, she went to extremes, becoming terror-struck at the onset of every childish ailment, dismissing nurses and governesses for trifling or imaginary offences, and keeping Valerie close to her at all times.

Perhaps because of the steadying presence of Valerie, the next few years were the most settled that Franz Josef and Elisabeth would experience together. The Empress was still often moody, and still kept most of the Court at a distance by surrounding herself with Hungarians, but she made a reasonable number of public appearances with her husband.

### Private and public duties

Franz Josef was able to share her company at Ischl, and enjoyed fox-hunting and family Christmases at Gödollo, the country mansion presented to Elisabeth by a grateful Hungarian nation. The situation was unaffected by the death in 1872 of the Archduchess Sophie, who had long since retreated to Ischl and lost her influence at court.

In 1873 Austria-Hungary held an Exhibition of Industry and Art, a type of event that had

## EMPEROR OF MEXICO

The first of the tragedies that struck down Franz Josef's family was the execution of his brother Maximilian. Although close to 'Max' in boyhood, Franz Josef came to distrust his restless, ambitious younger brother. Possibly, too, he disliked the friendship between Maximilian and another discontented soul, the Empress Elisabeth. Frustrated at home, Maximilian and his wife Carlotta, daughter of the King of The Belgians, accepted the Mexican throne in 1862. The pair were supported by France but when the French withdrew Maximilian was captured by rebels. A frantic Carlotta rushed to Europe to appeal for the assistance of Franz Josef and the Pope. When her efforts came to nothing, she went insane while staying in the Vatican, remaining institutionalized for the rest of her long life. The unfortunate Maximilian was executed by a firing squad in 1867 *above*

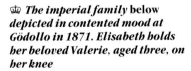

*The imperial family* below depicted in contented mood at *Gödollo in 1871. Elisabeth holds her beloved Valerie, aged three, on her knee*

carried enormous international prestige ever since the famous 1851 Great Exhibition in London. Acting as hosts to the Prince of Wales, the Tsar of Russia, the German Empress and numerous other rulers, Franz Josef and Elisabeth seemed an enviable couple. They carried out their duties impeccably, although the Empress was prostrated by nervous exhaustion when the proceedings at last came to an end.

This proved to be Elisabeth's last great effort to carry out her duties in conventional fashion. Despite the distractions of annual trips to Possenhofen, Ischl and Gödollo, she became increasingly nervous and restless. Moreover, Gisela had married, and in January 1874 gave birth to a daughter. Elisabeth, dedicated to her own rarefied beauty, found herself a grandmother at the age of 37 and seems to have felt an impulse to grasp at the last shadowy possibilities of romance.

### Elisabeth's search for love

In February 1874, during the Vienna Carnival, she went to a masked ball in disguise, and flirted with a young civil servant named Fritz

Interfoto

Popperfoto

Pacher. She then sent him a series of tantalizing letters, signed 'Gabrielle', from foreign parts. But when Pacher showed that he had a shrewd idea of their author's real identity, Elisabeth broke off the correspondence.

Her involvement with England – and with Captain George 'Bay' Middleton of the 12th Lancers – was much deeper. For eight years, from 1875 to 1882, the Empress spent long periods fox-hunting in England or Ireland, skimping the courtesies due to Queen Victoria and other notables, but captivating the hard-hunting nobles and gentry of the shires.

Beautiful, fearless, tireless and superbly skilled, she 'looked like an angel and rode like the devil'. For her, fox-hunting became a mania, but one unnoticed by her British admirers, who shared it. Outstanding among them was Bay Middleton, who began by being assigned to look after the Empress and went on to hunt with her each year in England and also, on the Emperor's invitation, at Gödollo.

Although Elisabeth surrounded herself with handsome men, Franz Josef seems never to have doubted her physical fidelity. And probably, given her fastidious, narcissistic temperament, he was right. However, her interests in Middleton certainly had a romantic element, for with his engagement to be married in 1882, Elisabeth's passion for England and fox-hunting came to an abrupt end.

### Rare moments of relaxation

Franz Josef was as devoted as ever to his wife, and also to the interests of state. His only escape from official duties was at Ischl, which he visited without fail every year. There he could put on his hunter's hat and leather shorts and go shooting in a state of blissful forgetfulness. He hunted chamois for preference, but also capercaillie and other kinds of game.

For the rest of the year, Franz Josef's life was dominated by the bureaucratic routine to which he had condemned himself. He rose from his simple truckle bed at 4 or 5 a.m., and spent most of the day at his desk. Thanks to his wife's diets, which kept her from the lunch table, he too rarely had a sit-down meal and would gulp down some homely dish while he worked. By 9 p.m. he was usually in bed.

♛ *Elisabeth's passion for hunting earned her the title of 'Queen of the Chase'. At various stages in her life, she pursued the sport, not only on her frequent visits to Ireland and England, but also at Gödollo above. Franz Josef preferred game shooting, often taking Crown Prince Rudolf with him on his trips to the Austrian Alps inset*

## 'She looked like an angel and rode like the devil'

COMMENT ON ELISABETH

# A LOVE ENSHRINED

*The Hofburg Palace is full of mementos of the love story of Franz Josef and Elisabeth. Portraits of the couple in oils, watercolour or porcelain cover the walls and fill the display cabinets, particularly in the rooms in which the Emperor spent most of his working life. Though Elisabeth spent little time in Vienna in the latter part of her life, her presence in the Palace is all-pervasive, a melancholy tribute to the longing which the Emperor forever felt, despite his string of misstresses, for the girl with whom he fell in love so many years before*

♛ Much fine porcelain was produced in mid 19th-century Vienna. Figure groups of the Emperor and his bride were particularly popular. The couple were modelled in many guises, including those of a hunter and a peasant girl *left*

♛ The rich red walls of Franz Josef's sleeping-chamber in the Hofburg *below* are hung with portraits of the teenage Elisabeth at Possenhofen and on horseback; alongside is a painting of the Emperor as a child with his mother

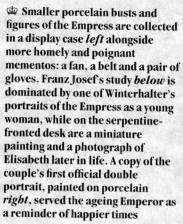

♛ Smaller porcelain busts and figures of the Empress are collected in a display case *left* alongside more homely and poignant mementos: a fan, a belt and a pair of gloves. Franz Josef's study *below* is dominated by one of Winterhalter's portraits of the Empress as a young woman, while on the serpentine-fronted desk are a miniature painting and a photograph of Elisabeth later in life. A copy of the couple's first official double portrait, painted on porcelain *right*, served the ageing Emperor as a reminder of happier times

Le Petit Journal

SUPPLÉMENT ILLUSTRÉ

S. M. L'IMPÉRATRICE ELISABETH D'AUTRICHE

# THE FINAL BLOWS

**WITH ELISABETH'S APPROVAL, THE EMPEROR FOUND COMFORT WITH HIS MISTRESSES, BUT FOR HER THERE WAS LITTLE HAPPINESS. FAMILY TRAGEDIES MULTIPLIED, EACH ONE EVEN MORE CRUSHING THAN THE LAST**

*☙ As the years went on, Elisabeth spent very little time with her husband in Vienna. Their relationship was carried on only through letters; wherever she was in her restless journeying about Europe, Elisabeth tried to write to him every day* right. *Despite – or perhaps because of – these long separations, the announcement of the premature death of the Empress* above *was a body blow to the ageing Emperor*

THE EMPEROR'S GRUELLING BUREAUCRATIC workload left him little time for relaxation. Although he may have had some mistresses-of-the-moment, Franz Josef's human needs were essentially domestic. In 1875 he began a liaison with a young woman who gave him the emotional and sexual comfort he needed.

Anna Heuduk, who was only 15 but married to an older man she hated, took to walking in the park at Schönbrunn until she attracted the Emperor's attention. Three years later she divorced her husband, and the Emperor arranged for her to marry a complaisant railway official named Nahowski.

Franz Nahowski, on orders from high places, was sent on a long tour of duty to Galicia and Franz Josef proceeded to set up Anna Nahowski in a villa near Schönbrunn. Here she gave him breakfast at 5 a.m. and, eventually, bore him a son and daughter. The Emperor's working day remained uninterrupted.

The relationship continued for until 1889, when Anna was summoned to the Palace. The Emperor's financial manager told her Franz Josef wished to discontinue the liaison. She was handed a sum of money in compensation but was not allowed to see the Emperor. She never spoke to him again.

Throughout this time there was still a bond between husband and wife. Franz Josef wrote regularly to Elisabeth, complaining of his loneliness and telling her of his longing for her. For her part, the Empress worried about him, wrote to him almost every day, and sent him souvenirs of her travels. But she was also realistic about the limitations of their relationship.

In 1884, when the Emperor began to show

## FRIEND IN THE WINGS

**Katherina Schratt** *right* **was a young actress who filled the void left in Franz Josef's life by the Empress Elisabeth's unwillingness to stay with him in Vienna. Elisabeth actually promoted the liaison, commissioning a portrait of Katherina from the court painter and arranging a meeting with the Emperor in the studio. Katherina was treated as 'the friend' by both Franz Josef and Elisabeth, and the two women even dieted together. Aware that she could never replace Elisabeth in Franz Josef's affections, Katherina maintained her independence, taking regular holidays by herself in Switzerland and the South of France. Finally, when she felt that the Emperor had let her down, she ended the relationship**

an interest in a plump, pretty actress at Vienna's Burgtheater, Elisabeth actively promoted the relationship. Katherina Schratt became Franz Josef's new breakfast companion, but also 'the friend' to whom the Empress sent her good wishes when she wrote to the Emperor. The favour shown by Elisabeth to Katherina gave her long relationship with the Emperor the ultimate seal of respectability.

## A restless life

In other respects, Elisabeth grew increasingly remote, eccentric and unhappy. Although painfully thin, she dieted on raw meat juices and oranges, and exercised relentlessly on gymnastic apparatus set up in her apartments. No longer a huntress, she relieved her terrible restlessness by walking for hours at a speed that wore out her ladies-in-waiting and the detectives whom Franz Josef assigned to guard her. The peasants of Corfu referred with admiration to the rapidly perambulating Empress as 'the locomotive'.

Her manias and fitful enthusiasms multiplied as she desperately sought for something to fill her life. She made a cult of the great German poet Heine, declaring that he had appeared to her in a vision. And she became obsessed with the culture of ancient Greece, learning the language and spending millions on Corfu. The money – supplied by the uncom-

### POETIC IDOL

The wit and lyrical genius of Heinrich Heine (1797-1856), one of Germany's greatest poets *right*, had a special appeal for the Empress Elisabeth. She filled the imperial Palaces with statues and busts of the poet. Her taste for literature was not shared by the Emperor, to whom Heine was just 'a subversive Jew'. Eventually Elisabeth's cult of Heine became obsessive. She claimed that he had appeared to her in a vision, and erected a temple dedicated to the poet in the garden of her pseudo-Greek palace, the Archilleion (now a casino), on the Greek island of Corfu

Mansell Collection

plaining Emperor – went on building a palatial 'ancient Greek' villa, the Achilleion, which she would ultimately abandon.

Meanwhile, there were shocks and disappointments. Elisabeth's cousin, King Ludwig II of Bavaria, became so eccentric that he was deposed and institutionalized. He later drowned in tragic circumstances. Elisabeth, who felt the affinity between their natures, defended Ludwig vehemently and even quarrelled about the matter with her family on a visit to Possenhofen.

The person she cared for most was her

👑 *The imperial Family only came together to pose for domestic portraits. The 1888 painting below shows (left to right) Archduchess Valerie, Empress Elisabeth, her grandaughter Elisabeth, the Emperor, Crown Prince Rudolf and his wife, Stephanie, and Archduchess Gisela with her husband and children. Soon after, the family was torn apart by the Mayerling tragedy*

Archiv Fur Kunst & Geschichte

daughter Valerie. 'I really love nobody but you,' she wrote. But Valerie was growing up and wanted to marry a young Habsburg prince. Although Elisabeth dreaded the separation, she loyally took her daughter's side when the Emperor tried to forbid the match.

### Mayerling tragedy

For a time all this was overshadowed by a truly appalling tragedy. Crown Prince Rudolf had grown up, married and become a father, and was popular with the Viennese as an elegant man about town and an outspoken liberal. Neither Rudolf's father, at odds with him politically, nor his remote, spasmodically affectionate mother suspected the existence of a Crown Prince who was addicted to morphia and obsessed with the idea of a suicide pact.

They were totally unprepared when the bodies of Rudolf and his mistress, Marie Vetsera, were discovered at Mayerling, the Prince's hunting lodge. At first it was believed that Rudolf had been poisoned by his mistress. Ironically, because no one dared tell Franz Josef, it was the neurotic, apparently frail Elisabeth who first heard the news and had to break it to her husband.

As at other moments of crisis, they stood together, although it was significant that Elisabeth soon sent for two sources of comfort – Katherina Schratt for the Emperor and Valerie for herself. After this, the Emperor took charge of the investigation of the Mayerling affair. He led the attempt to cover up the fact that Rudolf

♔ *The hunting lodge at Mayerling* above *was used by Crown Prince Rudolf* left *as a private retreat. His addiction to morphine aggravated his hereditary infirmity of mind and filled the young man with thoughts of suicide. In 1889 he took his latest mistress, the teenage Marie Vetsera, to the lodge and, in a locked bedroom, shot her, then took his own life*

♔ *The announcement of Rudolf's death* below *was delayed for a day to allow for a cover-up of the circumstances; as a murderer and suicide, he would never have received a Catholic burial. After Franz Josef made his farewells* left*, the Crown Prince, said to have died of heart failure, was given a state funeral*

44

had killed his mistress then committed suicide. The body of Marie Vetsera was spirited away and buried quietly, and it was announced that the Crown Prince had died of a heart attack.

Elisabeth was sent to Budapest, away from the unpleasant, often well-founded rumours about the deaths that were circulating in Vienna. When it was all over, the Empress, almost always dressed in black, continued to be consumed by grief and guilt. The Emperor had become an old man but, as was his wont, he gallantly soldiered on.

## Set in their ways

The pattern of the relationship between Franz Josef and Elisabeth was now fixed, and nothing but death would change it. From his desk the Emperor wrote to his wife, ' I think of you all the time with boundless longing, and am already looking forward to our next meeting, which is still so far away.'

Elisabeth flitted all round the Mediterranean and to Madeira, England and Biarritz, nev-

> ## 'An ill-fated, moonstruck creature whose chief inclination was to be majestically miserable'
>
> LEOPOLD OF TUSCANY ON ELISABETH

er finding rest or purpose. Her suffering was physical as well as psychological, and at spas and resorts she sought alleviation for her sciatica, and a cure for a rash that marred the remains of her beauty.

At least one of the younger generation, Prince Leopold of Tuscany, could now look at her without being dazzled. He saw her as 'an ill-fated, moonstruck creature whose chief inclination was to be majestically miserable.'

Yet although her miseries multiplied and she often claimed to long for death, Elisabeth — unlike her son — had a strength of character which prevented her collapsing under the blows of fate. Her health was in ruins, her favourite daughter Valerie had married, her mother and two of her sisters had died (typically, it was Franz Josef, not Elisabeth, who went to Ludovika's funeral) but Elisabeth survived.

She even found the strength to play the Empress again, entertaining the Tsar and Tsarina at the Hofburg and making one last, triumphant appearance with the Emperor at

Budapest. In 1898 – the year of the Emperor's Golden Jubilee – it seemed for a time that she might be dying, but a better diet and a cure at Bad Nauheim brought about a dramatic improvement in her health.

## A time of anarchy

Instead of dying, Elisabeth had to be killed. The 1890s were a time of anarchist outrages. Assassinations and acts of terrorism were carried out by seasoned conspirators and by crazed young men. One of the latter was a young Italian, Luigi Luccheni, who was working on the site of the new Lausanne post office. He dreamed of the

♛ *Though they were briefly brought together again by the death of their son, Franz Josef and Elisabeth soon went their separate ways again. The last picture ever taken of the two together* below *shows them striding purposefully through a park in one of Elisabeth's favourite spas, Bad Kissingen*

Ullstein

blow for freedom that he would someday strike with a home-made stiletto he had fashioned from a small file sharpened to a point. His plans were vague: his only fixed intention was to rid the world of the first crowned head or president who came within reach.

The Empress Elisabeth was staying at Caux in Switzerland, where there was a spa, when she received an invitation to lunch with Julie de Rothschild on her estate at Pregny, on the shores of Lake Geneva. She accepted, deciding that she would also take the opportunity to see something of Geneva itself. When warned that the city was a haven for terrorists, she laughed: 'Who would want to harm an old woman like me?' She was 60.

The Empress set out on 9 September 1898, travelling as the Countess of Hohenembs — one of her many incognitos. These aliases rarely deceived anyone about the true identity of the beautiful, imperious, black-clad eccentric who walked at such an extraordinary speed.

After a sumptuous meal at Pregny, Elisabeth returned to Geneva, looked about the town and stayed the night at a hotel. The following morning she bought her daughter Valerie a mechanical device for making music. At some time after 1 p.m, her lady-in-waiting, the Countess Sztáray, persuaded the rather lethargic Elisabeth to leave the hotel in a hurry so that they would not miss the steamer that would take them to Caux.

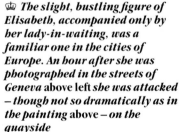
*The slight, bustling figure of Elisabeth, accompanied only by her lady-in-waiting, was a familiar one in the cities of Europe. An hour after she was photographed in the streets of Geneva* above left *she was attacked – though not so dramatically as in the painting* above *– on the quayside*

# STABBED

As the two women approached the quay, a man appeared to lurch into her. His hand flew up, and the Empress fell over. She was helped up, and insisted on going on board. As the steamer set off, she collapsed, and the Countess at first believed she had had a heart attack. Only when she opened the Empress's blouse did she see a tiny spot of blood and realize that her mistress had been wounded.

Although Luccheni had struck Elisabeth in the heart, his weapon was so narrow that its effects were not instantaneous. The steamer turned back, and Elisabeth was taken to her hotel, where she died about an hour after she had been assaulted.

Luccheni made no serious attempt to escape, but Genevan law denied him the martyrdom he had hoped for. He committed suicide after 12 years in prison.

## Despair

When the news reached Vienna, Franz Josef was in his room at Schönbrunn, writing at a desk in front of which hung a portrait of Elisabeth by the artist Winterhalter. In his despair at this final tragedy, he sobbed, 'Is nothing to be

♛ *Elisabeth's body was brought back to Vienna by train for a state funeral. Her coffin was paraded through the streets of the capital* above *on the night of 15 September; those Viennese who had once vilified the Empress for turning her back on them helped swell the crowds who bore silent witness to its passage*

♛ *After the death of her son, Elisabeth* left, *(portrayed in the year of her death) customarily wore mourning dress until the day she died. Her assassin, Luigi Luccheni* far left *had no personal grudge against the Empress, but espoused the Anarchist creed of Freedom through Action. In attacking the slight, ageing Elisabeth, he felt that he and his co-conspirators, who were never caught, were striking a blow against tyranny for oppressed peoples everywhere*

## VICTIM OF SARAJEVO

After the death of Crown Prince Rudolf at Mayerling, the Archduke Franz Ferdinand became the heir to the throne of Austria-Hungary. Although a more conventional figure than either Rudolf or the Empress, he too violated the Habsburg code by falling in love with a mere Countess and insisting on marrying her. He was permitted to do so, but the marriage had to be morganatic (Franz Ferdinand's children would be passed over in the succession to the throne). Given few responsibilities by the Emperor, the Archduke was allowed to make a State visit to Bosnia, where there was unrest among the Serb population. At Sarajevo, the capital, he and his wife *right* were shot dead by Serb conspirators – an event that set off the European crisis leading to World War 1

## THE LAST EMPEROR

A man of good will and bad luck, the Archduke Karl was thrust on to the stage of history by the assassination of the Habsburg heir-apparent Franz Ferdinand and the death of his great-uncle, the Emperor Franz Josef. The timing was unfortunate as Karl, still only 24, became Emperor of Austria-Hungary in November 1916. In the third year of the World War, the Empire was short of food and its various nationalities were restive. Karl, a man of peace, negotiated with the Allies but failed to bring Austria-Hungary out of the war. With defeat, the Empire disintegrated and in March 1919 the last Habsburg Emperor went into exile in Switzerland. After unsuccessful attempts to regain the throne of Hungary, Karl *right* died in Madeira in 1922

Mansell Collection

⚜ *Following the death of his wife, the Emperor lived out the remaining 18 years of his life much as he had lived the previous 50 – at his desk. In 1908, his Diamond Jubilee was marked by a reception at Schönbrunn below His reign of 68 years was one of the longest ever of any monarch*

Roger Viollet

spared me on this earth?' And then, to himself, 'No one will ever know how much I loved her.'

After Elisabeth's death, Franz Josef did as he had always done: he went on with his work, although with the years he grew greyer, balder and more humped with bending over a desk. For a time, Katherina Schratt was a great consolation, among other things because she was the only person with whom he could talk freely about their 'Adored One'.

Katherina, however, felt less at ease once the Empress was no longer on the scene to make the situation seem respectable. Perhaps, too, she was tiring of retailing amusing breakfast-time gossip to an elderly gentleman who had little light conversation to offer in return.

When Franz Josef took the view that it would be improper to help her persuade the Burgtheater to renew her contract, she broke off the relationship. The Emperor wrote a number of pathetic letters vainly begging her to reconsider. Even in these he could not refrain

# 'No one will ever know how much I loved her'

### FRANZ JOSEF ON ELISABETH

from asking her – perhaps not very tactfully – to 'remember the dear departed woman who we both loved, and who watches over us as a guardian angel.'

### End of the Empire

Seemingly indestructible, despite his years and sorrows, Franz Josef became the venerable Grand Old Man of the Empire. Even at 80 he was able to get into the saddle and review a parade in Bosnia.

He lived to see the assassination of his nephew and heir, Franz Ferdinand, at Sarajevo in 1914, and to see events run out of control and detonate a World War. On 21 November 1916, Franz Josef, who had guided the destiny of the Habsburg Empire for 68 years, died just two years before the end of the war that would destroy it.